This paperback edition first published in 2020

ISBN: 978-0–9955904-0-3
(Paperback)

Publishers Details

Company DIrector: Xavier P.

Contact: TSTACPublishing@gmail.com

written by

Xavier Pencel

illustrated by

Olaf Biró

TSTAG

Ocyrus had to stay inside today,
as it was pouring down with rain outside.

"No park today, son," said Daddy.

“I’m bored,” said Ocyrus,
as he peeked outside
with a long gloomy face.

"Hmm,
What are we going to do
with this paint?" said Daddy.

Aha, I know!" said Ocyrus.

"We can paint some
pictures with our
hands and feet.

So they began to dip their **HANDS** and **FEET** into the paint,

splatting,

plopping

and stamping

paint onto their paper.

"Oh no, look at all these cooking ingredients!" said Daddy.

"What are we going to do?"

"Aha, I know," said Ocyrus.

"We'll make wolf biscuits and then we'll gobble them all up."

So they cracked, poured and melted their ingredients into a bowl...

whisking, beating and churning their biscuit batter.

"Don't eat me!"
cried daddy.

"I'm the big, bad **PIG**!"
snorted Ocyrus.

“Oh no, look at this big box!” said Daddy.

“What are we going to do now?”

“Aha, I know,”
said Ocyrus.

“We’ll build a spaceship.”

So they started to snap, bend and fold the box...

as they cut out wings,
a seat and a window for a spaceship.

"3, 2, 1 lift off!" said Ocyrus,...

as they flew across space and
passed orbiting planets.

"Oh no, someone left their scuba goggles," said Daddy.
"What shall we do?"

"Aha, I know," said Ocyrus.

"We'll go scuba diving.

So they filled the bath up to the top, top, top and added some special bubbles.

"Look!
The giraffe is blowing bubbles,...

and the tiger
is popping them!" said Ocyrus.

"Oh no, look at all this mess!" said Mummy.

“What are we going to do now?”
said Daddy.

“Hmm. I'm sorry Daddy”
said Ocyrus.

“I'm too tired to think right now,” he said, as he let out a big yawn, before shutting his eyes tightly.

"Aha, I know," said Daddy.
"I think it's time for bed."

Ocyrus cuddled up with
his mommy, snuggling up
underneath the quilt, ...

smiling in bed
dreaming of all
the adventures
he went on that day.

"So who's gonna tidy up now?"
said Daddy,...

as he yawned
and stretched
his arms out wide.

So Mummy gave
him a pair of gloves
for washing up,
and a dustpan and brush
to sweep up.

So Daddy had to tidy up before bed.

THE END